THE CHILDREN'S BIBLE

Volume 2

A Golden Press / Funk & Wagnalls, Inc. Book
Published by Western Publishing Company, Inc.

Distributed by Funk & Wagnalls, Inc. New York

Library of Congress Catalog Card Number: 81-81439

ISBN 0-8343-0039-7 (Volume 2)
ISBN 0-8343-0037-0 (12 Volume Set)

CONTENTS

INTRODUCTION

In this volume you will read about Jacob and Joseph, both great leaders of God's chosen people. Jacob was the ruler of the Hebrews, a tribe of men and women who wandered throughout the land of Canaan in search of water and food for their flocks of sheep and goats. The Bible tells us that Jacob was Isaac's son and Abraham's grandson. Like these two great patriarchs, Jacob led his tribe as it moved from place to place. The people looked to him for advice and guidance.

Jacob's people were nomads, which means they had no permanent home, but moved in search of pasture for their flocks. They did not wander across the desert, but kept close to the towns in Canaan, because they depended on the towns for their supplies.

The Canaanite people, who lived in Canaan together with the Hebrew people, were great builders of towns. They built their towns and cities with very strong walls to protect themselves against invasion, and built secret tunnels for water so that no enemy could ever block their water supply. The Canaanites were also great traders who travelled as far away as Greece by ship to trade their goods. Among the things they traded was a beautiful purple dye which they invented. This dye was famous and was highly valued by the rich and powerful people in other lands because they could make beautiful cloth from it. Joseph's robe of many colors was made with the famous dyes of Canaan. The Canaanite people also developed an alphabet, which was one of the precursors of our own alphabet.

Although the Canaanites were like the Hebrew people in many respects — they lived in the same land and even spoke a similar language — they did not worship the same god. The Canaanites made little stone figures in the shapes of animals and people, and they worshipped these statues as their gods.

The land of Canaan was part of the great and powerful kingdom of Egypt, which was the ruling nation in the lands of the Bible at the time of Jacob and Joseph. Egypt had won control over all these lands partly because the Egyptians were fierce warriors. They were among the first people to use horse-drawn chariots, which allowed them to charge into battle and surround their enemies. Few armies could withstand the power of the Egyptian chariots.

Egypt was a great kingdom not only because of its wars, but because the pharaohs, who were the rulers and religious

leaders of Egypt, knew how to rule in times of peace. "Pharaoh" was the ruler's title, like "king" or "emperor." The Egyptian people believed that the pharaohs were gods as well as men — like the Canaanites, they practiced a different religion than the Hebrews.

Egypt is a desert land, except for the area along the banks of the river Nile. Every year the river overflows, leaving behind rich soil and minerals on the flood plain along its banks. The Egyptian people farmed on the fertile land along the Nile. Unlike the people of Canaan, who had to worry all the time about having enough water and rain, the Egyptian people could usually depend upon a steady supply of water from the Nile — although there were times when the Nile did not overflow and there was drought, or it overflowed too much and there was flooding.

In the years of good harvests, the pharaohs stored food away for the years when the Nile did not give the people the water they needed. In Canaan the people stored water in wells, and they were always looking for new ways to improve these wells so that they could hold more water for longer periods of time. Because the Nile River was a more reliable source of water than the wells in Canaan, the Hebrew people sometimes travelled into Egypt when they suffered from hunger or thirst. In the stories about Joseph and his brothers, the brothers went into Egypt because there was a drought and famine in Canaan.

The Hebrew people were not treated well in Egypt. Sometimes they could find work and food there, but the Egyptians did not like to see people entering their land from Canaan. The people of Canaan suffered because they were strangers in the land of Egypt. There was even a law in Egypt that said the Hebrews and the Egyptians could not eat at the same table.

The life of the Hebrew people, both when they were in Canaan and when they were in Egypt, was a hard life. They were a small group of peaceful shepherds who wandered all over lands ruled by mighty powers like Egypt. The Hebrew people had to struggle to find enough water and food for themselves and their animals, and often they had to endure hunger and thirst and sickness. Yet through all of this they kept their faith that God was guiding them, and they put their trust in him. This was not always easy for them to do, and at times they doubted. Perhaps when they were hungry, they wondered whether God had left them alone in the desert. Yet they always came back to their strong belief that God cared for them and was protecting them. They continued to worship their God as they wandered between Canaan and Egypt.

72

from the
BOOK OF GENESIS
Part 2

ESAU AND JACOB

ATER when Isaac was three score years old, Rebekah bore him twin sons. The firstborn had red hair all over like a hairy coat. They called him Esau. His brother they called by the name of Jacob.

The boys grew. Esau became a cunning hunter, a man of the out-of-doors, but Jacob was a plain man, dwelling in tents. Isaac loved Esau, because he liked to eat his venison, but Rebekah loved Jacob.

One day Jacob was boiling a thick soup, when Esau came from the field. Esau was faint with hunger and said to Jacob:

"Feed me, I pray you, some of that good lentil soup, for I am faint."

"Sell me this very day your birthright," said Jacob. For Esau, being the elder, was to inherit their father's goods.

"I am at the point of death," said Esau. "What good will this birthright do me?"

But Jacob said, "Swear to me this day."

So Esau swore to him, and sold his birthright to Jacob. Then Jacob gave Esau bread and the lentil soup. Esau ate and drank, then he rose up and went his way.

Thus Esau threw away his birthright.

REBEKAH AND JACOB PLOT AGAINST ISAAC

When Isaac was old, his eyes became dim, so that he could see no longer. He called Esau, his elder son, and said to him:

"My son."

"Here I am," said Esau.

"Look now," said Isaac, "I am old, I do not know the day of my death. Take your weapons, your quiver and your bow, go out to the field and get me some venison. Make me savory meat, such as I love, and bring it to me that I may eat, so that my soul may bless you before I die."

Now Rebekah was listening and heard what Isaac said to Esau, his son. Esau went to the field to hunt for the venison and to bring it home.

Then Rebekah spoke to Jacob her son, saying:

"Behold, I heard your father speak to Esau, your brother, saying, 'Bring me venison and make me savory meat, that I may eat, and bless you before the Lord before my death.' Now, therefore my son, obey my voice and do as I command you.

"Go now to the flock and fetch me from it two good kids of the goats, and I will make them into savory meat for your father, such as he loves. You shall take it to your father, that he may eat, and that he may bless you before his death."

Jacob said to Rebekah, his mother:

"Behold, Esau my brother is a hairy man, and I am a smooth man. Perhaps my father will feel me, and I shall seem a deceiver. I shall bring a curse upon myself, and not a blessing."

But his mother said to him:

"Upon me be the curse, my son. Only obey my voice and go fetch the kids to me that I may prepare them."

So he went and fetched them to his

mother, and his mother made a savory meat, such as his father loved.

Then Rebekah took the best robes of her elder son Esau, which were in the house, and put them upon Jacob her younger son. With the skins of the kids she covered his hands and the smooth of his neck.

Then she put into the hands of Jacob the savory meat, and the bread she had prepared.

So Jacob went to Isaac and said: "My father."

And Isaac said: "Here I am. Who are you, my son?"

"I am Esau, your firstborn," Jacob

said to his father. "I have done as you told me. Arise, I beg of you, sit up and eat of my venison, so that your soul may bless me."

But Isaac said to his son: "How is it that you found it so quickly, my son?"

"Because the Lord your God brought it to me," said Jacob.

Still Isaac said to Jacob:

"Come near, I beg of you, so that I may feel you, my son, and know whether you are really my son Esau or not."

Jacob went near to Isaac his father, and Isaac felt him and said:

"The voice is Jacob's voice, but the hands are the hands of Esau."

He did not recognize him, because his hands were hairy like the hands of Esau his brother, so he blessed him. Once more he said:

"Are you really my son Esau?"

"I am," said Jacob.

Then Isaac said: "Bring it near to me, and I will eat of my son's venison, that my soul may bless you."

Jacob brought the food close to him, and he ate. He brought him wine, and he drank.

Then Isaac said to him:

"Now, come near and kiss me, my son."

Jacob came near and kissed him. Isaac smelled the smell of his robe and blessed him, saying:

"See the smell of my son is as the smell of
a field which the Lord has blessed!

May God give you of the dew of heaven
and the fatness of the earth,
and plenty of corn and wine.

Let people serve you,
and nations bow down to you.

Be lord over your brothers.
and let your mother's sons bow down
to you.

May every one who curses you be cursed,
and blessed be those that bless you!"

Now it happened, as soon as Isaac had finished blessing Jacob, and when Jacob had scarcely left Isaac his father, that Esau his brother came in from his hunting. He also made savory meat and brought it to his father.

"My father," he said, "please rise up and eat of your son's venison, so that your soul may bless me."

Then Isaac his father said to him: "Who are you?"

"I am your son, your firstborn, Esau."

Then Isaac trembled all over and said:

"Who is he then, he who prepared venison and brought it to me, and I ate of it before you came and have blessed him? Yes, and he shall be blessed."

ISAAC DISCOVERS THE PLOT

When Esau heard the words of his father, he cried out with a great and bitter cry, and said to his father:

"Bless me, even me, also, O my father!"

But Isaac said:

"Your brother came with cunning and has taken away your blessing."

Esau said:

"Is he not rightly named Jacob, for he has taken my place twice? He took away my birthright, and, behold, now he has taken away my blessing."

Then he said: "Have you not saved a blessing for me?"

Isaac answered and said to Esau:

"Now, I have made him lord over you, and all his brothers I have given to him for servants. I have provided him with corn and wine. What is there I can do for you, my son?"

Esau said to his father:

"Have you only one blessing, my father? Bless me also, O my father!"

Esau lifted up his voice and wept. Then Isaac his father answered and said to him:

"Behold, your dwelling shall be far from the
fatness of the earth,
and far from the dew of heaven from above.
By your sword shall you live,
and shall serve your brother;

Then, it shall come to pass when you shall
have power,
That you shall break his yoke from off your
neck!"

Therefore Esau hated Jacob, because of the blessing with which his father had blessed him, and Esau said in his heart: "The days of mourning for my father are near. Then I will slay my brother Jacob."

These words of Esau, Rebekah's elder son, were told her and she sent for Jacob, her younger son.

"Now your brother Esau," she said to him, "wants to be revenged upon you and kill you. Therefore, my son, obey my voice and rise, flee to Laban, my brother, at Haran. Stay with him a few days, until your brother's fury turns away from you and he forgets what you have done to him. I will send and fetch you home again."

Isaac called Jacob, and blessed him. Then he commanded him, saying:

"You shall not take a wife among the daughters of Canaan. Arise, go to Padan-Aram, to the house of Bethuel, your mother's father, and take a wife there from among the daughters of Laban, your mother's brother. God Almighty bless you, that you may inherit the land where you are a stranger and which God gave to Abraham."

And Isaac sent Jacob away.

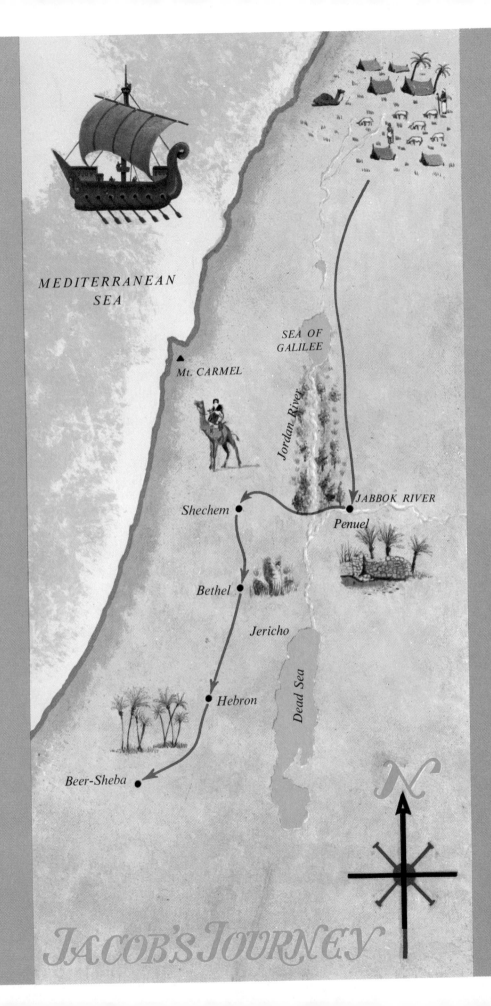

MEDITERRANEAN
SEA

SEA OF
GALILEE

Mt. CARMEL

Jordan River

JABBOK RIVER

Shechem

Penuel

Bethel

Jericho

Dead Sea

Hebron

Beer-Sheba

N

JACOB'S JOURNEY

JACOB'S FLIGHT AND DREAM

ACOB set out from Beersheba and started towards Haran. He came to a certain place and had to stay there all night, because the sun had set. Taking one of the stones from the ground, he placed it under his head for his pillow, and lay down in that place to sleep.

Jacob dreamed, and in his dream he saw a ladder set up on the ground, the top reaching to heaven, and, behold, angels of God were going up and down on it.

The Lord was standing above the ladder and he said to Jacob:

"I am the Lord God of Abraham, and the God of Isaac. The land on which you lie I will give to you and your children. Your children shall be as the dust of the earth and you will spread abroad to the west and to the east, to the north and to the south. Through you and your children all the families of the earth will be blessed.

"Behold, I am with you, and I will guard you everywhere you go, and will bring you back to this place. For I will not leave you until I have done everything I have promised."

Then Jacob waked out of his sleep and said:

"Surely the Lord is in this place, and I did not know it." He was afraid and said:

"This is surely the house of God, and this is the gate of heaven."

Early in the morning Jacob rose up,

took the stone that he had used as a pillow, set it up for a pillar and poured oil upon the top of it. He called the name of that place Bethel.

Then Jacob vowed a vow, saying:

"If God will be with me, and will guard me in the journey I am undertaking, and will give me bread to eat and clothes to wear, if I return again to my father's house in peace, then the Lord will be my God. This stone, which I have set up for a pillar, will be God's house, and of all that you give to me, O God, I will give a tenth to you."

JACOB AND RACHEL

 ACOB went on his journey and came into the land of the people of the East. As he looked he saw a well in a field and three flocks of sheep lying by it. It was the well from which the flocks were watered and a great stone was upon its mouth. When all the flocks were gathered around it, the shepherds would roll the stone from the well's mouth, water the sheep, and then put the stone back upon the well's mouth.

Jacob said to the shepherds:

"My brothers, where are you from?"

"We are from Haran," they said.

"Do you know Laban, the son of Nahor?" he asked them.

They said:

"We know him."

"Is all well with him?" Jacob said.

They said, "All is well with him, and, see, there is Rachel, his daughter, coming with the sheep."

While they were talking, Rachel came with her father's sheep, for she looked after them. And when Jacob saw Rachel, the daughter of Laban, his mother's brother, and saw Laban's sheep, he rolled away the stone which covered the well's mouth and watered the flock of Laban.

Then Jacob kissed Rachel and lifted up his voice and wept. He told Rachel that he was her father's kin and Rebekah's son. And leaving the sheep, Rachel ran and told her father.

Laban hastened out to meet Jacob,

"Because you are my kin, should you work for me for nothing? Tell me, what shall your wages be?"

Now Laban had two daughters. The name of the elder was Leah, and the name of the younger was Rachel. Leah was plain, but Rachel was very beautiful and pleasing to look upon.

Jacob loved Rachel, so he said:

"I will work for you seven years if at the end of that time you give me Rachel, your younger daughter."

Then Laban said: "It is better that I give her to you than to any other man. Stay with me."

So Jacob served seven years for Rachel, and they seemed to him but a few days, because he loved her.

his sister's son, and embraced him, kissed him, and brought him to his house. Jacob told Laban all the things that had happened to him, and Laban said to him: "Surely you are my bone and flesh."

And when Jacob had stayed with him for a month, Laban said to him:

JACOB SEEKS TO LEAVE LABAN

At the end of the seven years, Jacob said to Laban:

"Give me my wife, for I have fulfilled our agreement." And Laban prepared a wedding feast. But that evening in the darkness, Laban brought Leah to Jacob, and he married her, believing she was Rachel. When Jacob discovered that he had been deceived, he said to Laban:

"What have you done to me? Did I not serve you for Rachel?"

Laban said:

"In our land it is not right to marry off the younger before the firstborn. But if you will promise to serve me yet seven years more, I will give you Rachel, too, as a wife."

So Jacob took Rachel as his wife also, as it was the custom in that time for a man to have more than one wife.

He served Laban seven more years. And he loved Rachel more than Leah.

Rachel did not bear any children and was unhappy. But Leah gave Jacob many sons. Then the Lord took pity on Rachel and allowed her to bear a son. And she named her son Joseph.

After twenty years with Laban, Jacob had prospered exceedingly. He had many cattle, and menservants and maidservants, and camels and asses. But he heard the words of Laban's sons, saying:

"Jacob has taken away all that was our father's, and from our father he has gotten all his wealth."

Jacob also saw that Laban was not the same toward him as before. And the Lord said to him:

"Return unto the land of your fathers, to your own land, and I will be with you."

So Jacob called Rachel and Leah

JACOB AND RACHEL DEPART

And when the time came for him to leave, Jacob stole away secretly while Laban was shearing his sheep. He passed over the river, fleeing with all that he possessed, and set his face toward Mount Gilead. On the third day, Laban was told that Jacob had fled. He took his brothers with him, and pursued Jacob for seven days and overtook him on Mount Gilead.

But God came to Laban the Syrian in a dream by night and said to him:

"Take heed that you speak not to Jacob, neither good nor bad."

Jacob had pitched his tent on the mount and Laban and his brothers pitched their tents close by. Then Laban came to Jacob and said: "What have you done? Why did you steal away without my knowledge and carry away my daughters, like war captives? Why did you not tell me so that I could send you on your way with merriment, with tambourines and with harps? You did not allow me even to kiss my grandsons and daughters goodbye. In so doing, you have behaved foolishly. It is in my power to harm you, but the God of your father spoke to me last night, saying: 'Take heed not to speak to Jacob, good or bad.' Now if you left because you are longing to return to your father's house, why then have you stolen my family images?"

Jacob did not know that Rachel had stolen Laban's images, and he answered:

"Search the tents and whatever you may find belonging to you, take it. And if anyone has stolen your family images, let that one not live."

So Laban searched Jacob's tent and the servants' tents, but he did not find the images. Rachel had hidden the images in the trappings of her camel and was sitting upon them. Laban

to the field, where he was with his flock and said to them:

"I see from your father's face that he no longer regards me as he did, but the God of my fathers has been with me. And you know that I have served your father with all my power. Yet your father has cheated me and changed my wages ten times, but never has God allowed him to do me harm.

"The angel of God spoke to me in a dream and said: 'I am the God of Bethel where you anointed the pillar and where you vowed a vow to me. Now arise, go out from this country and return to your own land.' "

Rachel and Leah answered and said to him: "Whatever God has said to you, do."

So Jacob rose up and set his sons and his wives upon camels and he took all his cattle and all his goods, to return to Isaac his father in the land of Canaan.

searched her tent but did not find the images, and Rachel said to her father:

"Let it not displease you that I do not rise in your presence, but I am not feeling well today."

Then Jacob became angry and chided Laban, saying:

"What wrong have I done against you, what sin have I committed that you should pursue me? You have searched all my belongings, but what have you found that was yours? Let it be set down here before my brothers and your brothers and let them judge between us. For twenty years I have been with you: your ewes and your she-goats have done well, and never have I eaten a ram from your flocks. The heat consumed me during the day and the cold by night. Sleep departed from my eyes. I served you fourteen years for your two daughters, and six years more for your cattle, and you have changed my wages ten times.

"Had you not feared the God of my father, the God of Abraham and Isaac, surely you would have sent me away now empty-handed. God has seen my suffering and the labor of my hands, and he rebuked you last night."

Laban answered and said to Jacob:

"These daughters are my daughters, these children are my children, these cattle are my cattle, and all that you see is mine.

"What could I do against my daughters and the children they have borne? Therefore, come, let us make a covenant, and let it be for a witness between you and me."

JACOB AND LABAN MAKE A PACT

Jacob took a stone and set it up for a pillar. Then Jacob said to the men with him:

"Gather stones and make a heap."

They did so and there they ate, upon the heap. Then Laban said:

"Behold this heap and behold this pillar, which I have cast between me and you. This heap is a witness between us. I will not pass over this heap to you, and you shall not pass over this heap to harm me. The God of Abraham and the God of Nahor judge between us."

Jacob swore by the fear of his father Isaac. Then he offered sacrifice upon the mount and called his brethren to eat bread, and they ate and tarried all night on the mount.

Early in the morning Laban rose and kissed his sons and his daughters and blessed them. He departed and returned to his land.

JACOB SENDS MESSENGERS TO ESAU

Jacob went on his way and the angels of God met him.

When he saw them, Jacob said: "This is God's host."

Then Jacob sent messengers before him to Esau, his brother, in the country of Edom. He commanded them, saying: "Thus you shall speak to my lord Esau: 'Your servant Jacob wishes to say to him that he has stayed with Laban until now. He has oxen, asses, flocks, menservants and woman-servants. He is sending to tell this to my lord, that he may find grace in his sight.'"

Later, the messengers returned to Jacob, saying: "We went to your brother Esau, and he is coming to meet you, and four hundred men are with him."

Jacob was greatly afraid and was distressed. He divided into two camps the people that were with him, the flocks, the herds and the camels, saying: "If Esau should come upon one camp and smite it, then the other camp shall be able to escape."

Then Jacob said:

"Deliver me, I pray you, O God, from the hands of my brother, from the hands of Esau, for I fear him lest he will come and strike me, sparing neither mother nor children. Yet you have said to me: 'I will surely do you good, and make your race as the sand of the sea, which cannot be numbered because of its multitude.' "

Jacob spent the night there; then he took from his possessions at hand a present for Esau, his brother: twenty goats and two hundred she-goats, twenty rams and two hundred ewes, thirty milking camels and their young, ten bulls and forty cows, twenty asses and ten colts.

He delivered them to his servants, keeping each drove separate from others. Then he said to the first servant:

"When Esau, my brother, meets you and asks: 'To whom do you belong? Where are you going? And to whom belong these beasts before you?' you will answer: 'They belong to your servant Jacob. They are a present for my lord Esau, and, behold, your servant is behind us.' "

Jacob gave the same order to the second servant, then to the third one, and to all those that were walking behind the droves, saying:

"This is how you will speak to Esau when you meet him."

For Jacob thought:

"I will appease him with the gift that goes ahead of me, and later I will look at his face. Perhaps he will accept me."

The men left with the present, and Jacob spent that night in the camp.

During the night Jacob rose up and took his two wives and his two women servants, together with his eleven sons, and passed over the ford of Jabbok. He sent them over the brook, with everything he owned.

Then Jacob was left alone. All night long he wrestled with an angel. At daybreak the angel said:

"Your name shall no longer be called Jacob but Israel, for you have contended with God and prevailed."

JACOB AND ESAU
ARE REUNITED

Jacob lifted up his eyes and, behold, Esau was coming, and with him were four hundred men. Jacob divided the children between Leah, Rachel and the two handmaids. He put the handmaids and their children foremost, Leah and her children came after, and Rachel and Joseph were last.

He went ahead of them and bowed himself to the ground seven times until he was near his brother. Esau ran to meet him, embraced him, and fell on his neck and kissed him, and they wept. Esau looked up and saw the women and the children.

"Who are those with you?" he said.

"Those are the children," Jacob said, "which God has graciously given your servant."

Then the handmaids came near, they and their children, and they bowed themselves. And then Joseph and Rachel came near, and they bowed themselves.

"What do you mean," Esau said, "by all this flock and cattle that I met?"

"These are to find grace in the sight of my lord," Jacob said.

"I have enough, my brother," Esau said. "Keep what is yours for yourself."

"No, I pray you," said Jacob, "if now I have found grace in your sight, then receive my present at my hand, for I have seen your face as

He urged him, and Esau took it and said:

"Let us go and start our journey. I will go before you."

"My lord knows," said Jacob, "that children are tender, and I have the care of ewes and milking cows with their young. Should they be overdriven, even one day, all the flocks will die.

"Let my lord, I pray, go ahead before his servant, and I will follow softly, in step with the cattle before me, and according to what the children are able to endure, until I come to my lord in Seir."

Esau said: "Then let me leave with you some of the men that are with me."

"What need is there?" said Jacob, "Just let me find grace in the sight of my lord."

So Esau departed that day on his way to Seir.

And Jacob went to Shalem, which is in the land of Canaan, and he pitched his tent outside of the city.

He bought the parcel of land, where he had spread his tent, for one hundred pieces of money. There he erected an altar, and called it El-elohe-Israel.

though I had seen the face of God, and you were pleased with me.

"Take, I pray you, the gift that was brought to you, because God has dealt graciously with me, and I have enough."

JOSEPH AND HIS BROTHERS

OW Jacob dwelt in the land where his father had been a stranger, in the land of Canaan. His son Joseph, now a strong and healthy lad, daily fed the flock with all his brothers, the sons of his father's wives. And Joseph brought his father an evil report of them.

Jacob loved Joseph more than all his sons, because he was the son of his old age, so he made for him a coat of many colors.

When his brothers saw that their father loved Joseph more than all his brothers, they hated him, and could not speak to him in a friendly way.

Joseph dreamed a dream and told it to his brothers, and they hated him all the more.

He said to them:

"Hear, now, this dream which I have dreamed. We were in the field binding sheaves, and, lo, my sheaf arose and stood upright, and your sheaves stood around about and bowed down to my sheaf."

Then his brothers said to him:

"Would you indeed be king over us? Would you really rule over us?"

They hated him all the more on account of his dreams, and on account of his words.

He dreamed another dream, and told it to his brothers:

"Behold, I have dreamed another dream," he said. "The sun, the moon

JOSEPH'S BROTHERS ARE ENVIOUS

His brothers were envious of him, but his father remembered the dream.

Now his brothers went to feed their father's flock in Shechem. And one day Jacob said to Joseph:

"Your brothers are feeding the flock in Shechem. Come, I will send you to them."

"Here I am," said Joseph.

"Go, then," said Jacob, "and see whether all is well with your brothers and the flocks, and bring me word again."

So he sent Joseph out of the valley of Hebron, and the boy arrived at Shechem. He was wandering in the field when a certain man found him and asked him:

"What are you looking for?"

"I am looking for my brothers," he said. "Can you tell me where they are feeding the flocks?"

"They went on from here," the man said, "for I heard them say, 'Let us go to Dothan.'"

So Joseph went after his brothers and found them in Dothan.

When they saw him far off, even before he came close to them, they plotted against him and wanted to slay him. They said to one another:

"Behold, here comes the dreamer. Come, now, let us kill him and throw him into a pit. We will say some wild beast has devoured him. Then we shall see what will become of his dreams!"

But Reuben heard this, and he said:

"Let us not kill him. Shed no blood. Throw him into this pit here in the wilderness, but do not lay hands on him."

He planned to save Joseph from their hands and to deliver him to his father again.

and the eleven stars bowed down to me."

He told the dream to his father, and his father rebuked him, saying:

"What is this dream you have dreamed? Shall your mother and I and your brothers really come to bow ourselves down to the earth before you?"

JOSEPH IS THROWN
INTO THE PIT

So it happened that when Joseph came up to his brothers, they stripped Joseph out of his coat, his coat of many colors which he was wearing. Then they took him and threw him into the pit. The pit was empty and there was no water in it.

Then they sat down to eat bread, but when they lifted their eyes, behold, they saw a caravan of Ishmaelites arriving from Gilead, their camels loaded with spices, balm and myrrh which they were carrying down to Egypt.

Then Judah said to his brothers:

"What will we gain if we kill our brother and conceal his blood? Come, let us sell him to the Ishmaelites, and let us not touch him, for he is our brother and our flesh."

This satisfied the brothers. They lifted Joseph out of the pit and sold him to the Ishmaelites for twenty pieces of silver, and the merchants took Joseph to Egypt.

When Reuben returned to the pit, behold, Joseph was no longer in the pit. Reuben tore his clothes in grief.

Then he went to his brothers and said: "The child is not there, and I, where shall I go?"

The brothers took Joseph's coat, killed a young goat, and dipped the coat in the blood. Then they brought the coat of many colors to their father, saying: "We found this. Do you know whether or not it is your son's coat?"

He recognized it and said:

"It is my son's coat. A wild beast has devoured him. Joseph has been torn in pieces."

Then Jacob tore his clothes in grief, and put on sackcloth and mourned for his son many days. All his sons and all his daughters rose up to comfort him, but he refused to be comforted, and said: "I will go down to the grave, mourning for my son."

Thus his father wept for him.

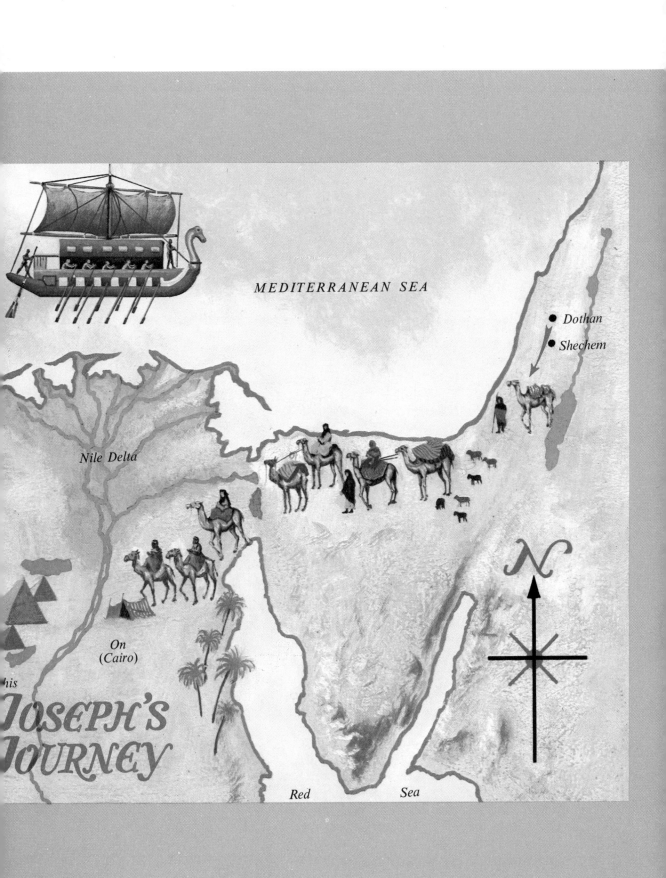

MEDITERRANEAN SEA

● Dothan

● Shechem

Nile Delta

On
(Cairo)

his

JOSEPH'S
JOURNEY

Red   Sea

N

JOSEPH IN EGYPT

JOSEPH was brought down to Egypt, and Potiphar, who was an officer of Pharaoh and captain of the guard, bought him from the Ishmaelites.

The Lord was with Joseph, and he became a favored servant, living in the house of his Egyptian master. His master saw that the Lord was with him, and that the Lord made all that he did prosper in his hands. Joseph found grace in his master's sight and he was made overseer in his house, and all that his master had he put in Joseph's hands.

The Lord blessed the Egyptian's house for Joseph's sake, and the blessing of the Lord was upon all that he had in the house and in the field. So Potiphar left all that he had to Joseph's hands, and he did not even know what he owned, except the bread he ate.

Now Joseph was a handsome young lad, and when he grew up his master's wife cast her eyes upon Joseph and loved him. But he would not love her, and said to her:

"Behold, my master does not even know what is in his house. He entrusted all that he has to my hand. There is none greater in this house than I. Neither has he kept back anything from me but you, because you are his wife. How then could I love you and do this great wickedness, and sin against God?"

Then she went to Joseph's master, and told lies about Joseph, saying:

"The Hebrew servant, whom you have brought to us, came into the house to mock me, and he fled as I lifted my voice and cried."

When the master heard the words of his wife, he was angry and he took Joseph and put him in prison, where the king's prisoners were kept, and there he stayed.

But the Lord was with Joseph and

showed him mercy, and made the keeper of the prison think well of him. So the keeper of the prison put all the prisoners that were in the prison into Joseph's hands, and whatsoever they did there, he was in charge of them.

The keeper of the prison paid no attention to anything that Joseph did, because the Lord was with Joseph, and whatever he did, the Lord made it prosper.

THE BUTLER'S DREAM

Some time later, it happened that the butler of the king of Egypt and his baker offended their Lord Pharaoh, the king of Egypt. In his anger, Pharaoh put them into the house of the captain of the guard, into the prison where Joseph was held. The captain of the guard turned them over to Joseph and he looked after them. They stayed in prison for some time.

Now one night, both the butler and the baker of the King of Egypt dreamed a dream, each of them a different dream. When Joseph came in to them in the morning and looked upon them, he saw that they were sad, he said to the men:

"Why do you look so sad today?"

"We have dreamed a dream," they said to him, "and there is no one to interpret it for us."

"Interpretations come from God," Joseph said to them. "Tell me your dreams."

So the chief butler told his dream to Joseph.

"In my dream," he said, "a vine was before me, and on the vine were three branches. It seemed as though it budded and the blossoms shot forth and the clusters grew into ripe grapes. Pharaoh's cup was in my hand. So I took the grapes and pressed them into Pharaoh's cup, and I placed the cup into the hand of Pharaoh."

Joseph said to him:

"This is the interpretation of your dream: The three branches are three days. Within three days Pharaoh will lift your head, he will restore you to your place, and you will place Pharaoh's cup into his hand, as you used to do when you were his butler.

"Only think of me and it shall be well with you, and be kind to me, I beg of you, and mention me to Pharaoh, and get me out of this place. For indeed I was stolen away from the land of the Hebrews, and I have done nothing here to deserve this dungeon."

THE BAKER'S DREAM

When the chief baker saw that the interpretation was good, he said to Joseph:

"I also had a dream and, behold, I had three baskets of white bread on my head. In the uppermost basket there were all kinds of baked goods for Pharaoh, and the birds ate them out of the basket upon my head."

Joseph answered him and said:

"This is the interpretation of your dream: The three baskets are three days. Within three days Pharaoh will call you and hang you on a tree, and the birds will eat your flesh."

On the third day, which was his birthday, Pharaoh made a feast for all the servants. He called for the butler and the chief baker among his servants. Then he returned the chief butler to the butlership again, and the butler gave the cup to Pharaoh. But Pharaoh hanged the chief baker, as Joseph had said.

Yet the chief butler did not remember Joseph but forgot him.

PHARAOH'S DREAMS

WO full years went by, and then it happened one night that Pharaoh dreamed. He stood by the river and, behold, seven fine, fat cows came out of the Nile and they fed in the meadow. Then, behold, seven other cows, thin and scrawny, came up after them out of the Nile and stood by the other cows upon the brink of the river, and the thin and scrawny cows ate up the seven fat and handsome cows. Then Pharaoh awoke.

He slept again and dreamed a second dream. Seven ears of corn came up on one stalk. They were hardy and good and, behold, seven ears, undersized and blasted by the east wind, sprang up after them, and the seven undersized ears swallowed the seven hardy and full ears. Pharaoh awoke and knew it was a dream.

On the next morning, his spirit was disturbed. He sent and called for all the magicians of Egypt, and the wise men of the land. Pharaoh told them his dreams, but there was no one who could interpret them to Pharaoh.

Then the chief butler spoke to Pharaoh, saying:

"Now I remember my faults. Pharaoh was angry with his servants and put me into the prison of the captain of the guard, both me and the chief baker. One night we each had a dream, he and I, each a different dream. There was in the prison with us a young man, a Hebrew, servant to the captain of the guard. We told him our dreams and he interpreted them to us, giving to each of us the meaning of our dreams. And everything happened as he told us, so it did. I was restored to my office, and the baker was hanged."

Then Pharaoh sent for Joseph. They brought him hastily out of the dungeon. He shaved himself, changed his clothing, and came to Pharaoh.

Pharaoh said to Joseph:

"I have had a dream and there is no one that can interpret it. I have heard it said that you can understand a dream and tell its meaning."

Joseph answered Pharaoh, saying:

"It is not in my power. God shall give Pharaoh an answer."

PHARAOH TELLS JOSEPH
HIS DREAMS

So Pharaoh said to Joseph:

"In my dream, behold, I stood upon the bank of the Nile, and there came out of the river seven cows, fat and handsome, and they fed in the meadow but, behold, seven other cows came up after them, thin and scrawny, such as I never saw in the land of Egypt for badness. The lean and scrawny cows ate the first seven cows, the fat ones, and when they had eaten them, they still appeared the same. They remained thin and scrawny as in the beginning. So I awoke.

"In my other dream I saw, behold, seven ears of corn come up on one stalk. They were full and good. Then, behold, seven ears, withered, thin and blasted with the east wind, sprung up after them. The thin ears devoured the seven good ears. I told these dreams to the magicians, but they could not interpret them for me."

Joseph said to Pharaoh:

"The two dreams of Pharaoh are one. God has shown Pharaoh what he is about to do.

"The seven good cows are seven years, and the seven good ears are seven years: the dream is the same. The seven thin and scrawny cows that came after are seven years, and the seven empty ears, blasted with the east wind, will be seven years of famine.

"This is the meaning of what I have told Pharaoh: What God is about to do, he is showing to Pharaoh. Behold, there will be seven years of great plenty throughout the whole land of Egypt. And after them will come seven years of famine. All the plenty shall be forgotten in the land of Egypt, and the famine shall consume the land. The plenty will no longer be remembered in the land because of the famine that will follow, for it shall be great.

"The dream was sent to Pharaoh twice because this thing has been decided by God, and God will make it happen soon.

"Now, therefore, let Pharaoh search for a man wise and discreet, and make him a governor over the land of Egypt. Let Pharaoh do this and let him appoint officers over the land, and gather up a fifth of the harvest of the land in the seven years of plenty.

98

"Let them gather all the food of those good years that come, and lay up corn under the order of Pharaoh, and keep it in the cities. And that food shall be stored for the land to draw on during the seven years of famine which shall come later in the land of Egypt, so that the land may not perish through famine."

The plan seemed good in the eyes of Pharaoh, and in the eyes of all his servants. Pharaoh said to his servants:

"Can we find such a man, a man in whom there is, as in this one, the spirit of God?"

PHARAOH REWARDS JOSEPH

Then Pharaoh said to Joseph:

"Inasmuch as God has shown you all this, there is no one as wise and as discreet as you are. You shall be in charge of my house, and all my people will be ruled according to your word. Only on the throne itself will I be greater than you." Then Pharaoh said to Joseph: "See, I have set you over all the land of Egypt."

Pharaoh took off the ring from his hand and put it upon Joseph's hand. He dressed him in robes of fine linen and put a gold chain around his neck. He made him ride in the second royal chariot, and people cried before him: "Bow the knee!" So Pharaoh made him ruler over all the land of Egypt, and he said to Joseph:

"I am Pharaoh, and without you no man shall lift up his hand or foot in all the land of Egypt. Then Pharaoh gave Joseph the Egyptian name of Zaphnath-paaneah and he gave him for his wife Asenath, the daughter of Potipherah, priest of On.

JOSEPH HAS SONS: MANASSEH AND EPHRAIM

Joseph was thirty years old when he stood before Pharaoh, king of Egypt. Then Joseph left Pharaoh, and went all over the land of Egypt. In the seven years of plenty, the earth brought forth food in abundance. So during those seven years when plenty

prevailed in the land, Joseph gathered up food and stored the food in the cities. In the same way, he stored up the food of the fields which closely surrounded the cities.

Joseph gathered grain in quantities as great as the sand of the sea: so much that he stopped counting, for it was without number.

Asenath the daughter of Potipherah, priest of On, gave Joseph two sons before the years of famine.

Joseph called the first Manasseh: "Because God," he said, "has made me forget all my suffering, and all my father's house."

And the name of the second was Ephraim: "Because God has made me

fruitful in the land of my affliction."

Then the seven years of plenty in the land of Egypt were ended, and the seven years of poverty began, just as Joseph had said. Famine was in all lands, but in all the land of Egypt there was bread. Then the land of Egypt was famished, and the people cried to Pharaoh for bread and he said to all the Egyptians:

"Go to Joseph, and do as he tells you."

The famine spread all over the face of the earth and Joseph opened all the storehouses and sold food to the Egyptians. The famine was severe in Egypt, but the famine was so severe in other lands that people from all countries came to Egypt to buy food from Joseph.

JOSEPH'S BROTHERS IN EGYPT

ACOB heard that there was grain in Egypt and he said to his sons:

"Why do you sit and look at one another? I have heard that there is grain in Egypt. Go down and buy some for us there, so that we may live and not die."

So Joseph's ten brothers set out to buy grain in Egypt. But Benjamin, Joseph's youngest brother, did not go with them, 'for harm might befall him,' said Jacob.

So, among the crowds that came to buy grain, came the sons of Jacob, for the famine was in the land of Canaan. Now Joseph was governor of the land. He sold grain to all the people of the land. Joseph's brothers came to him and bowed themselves before him with their faces to the earth.

When Joseph saw his brothers, he recognized them, but he acted as a stranger toward them and he spoke roughly to them, saying:

"Where did you come from?"

"From the land of Canaan to buy food," they said.

Joseph's brothers did not know him, but he remembered the dreams he had dreamed of them, and he said to them:

"You are spies. It is to find out the secret of this land that you have come."

"No, my lord," they said to him, "your servants have come only to buy food. We are true men, your servants are not spies."

And Joseph said to them:

"No, you have come to find out the secrets of the land."

"We are twelve brothers," they said, "the sons of one man in the land of Canaan. The youngest one is with our father now, and one is no more."

But Joseph said again:

"It is just as I said: You are spies. This shall be the proof: By the life of Pharaoh, you shall not go out of here unless your youngest brother comes to this place. Send one of you and let him fetch your brother, and you shall be kept in prison so that it may be proved whether there is any truth in your words. Or else, by the

life of Pharaoh, surely you are spies."

And he put them all together under guard for three days.

The third day Joseph said to them:

"Do this and save your lives, for I am a God-fearing man. If you are true men, let one of you stay bound in the prison where you are kept. The rest of you take grain to feed the hungry in your houses. But bring your brother to me, the youngest one, so that your words are proven, and you shall not die."

And they did so, saying to one another: "Truly we are guilty about our brother, for we saw the anguish of his soul when he pleaded with us, and we would not listen. That is why this distress has come upon us."

And Reuben answered them:

"Did I not tell you: Do not sin against the child? But you would not listen and now we must settle for his blood."

They did not know that Joseph understood them, for he spoke to them through an interpreter. Joseph turned away from them and wept. Then he returned and spoke to them. He took Simeon from them and bound him before their eyes.

Then Joseph ordered servants to fill their sacks with grain, to put every man's money back into his sack, and to give them provisions for the journey. That was how he treated them.

THE BROTHERS RETURN HOME

So they loaded their asses with the grain and started home. But when they stopped at an inn and one of them opened his sack to feed his ass, he spied his money in the mouth of his sack.

"My money is back in my sack!" he said to his brothers.

Their hearts failed them and they were afraid, saying to one another:

"What is this that God has done to us?"

They came home to Jacob, their father, in the land of Canaan, and told him all that had happened.

"The man, who is the lord of the land, treated us harshly and took us for spies, but we said to him: 'We are true men, we are not spies. We were twelve brothers. One is no longer, and the youngest is with our father in the land of Canaan.' Then the man who is the lord of the land said to us:

" 'I will know if you are true men. Leave one of your brothers here with me and take food to feed the hungry in your houses, and be gone. Then bring your brother to me, the youngest, and I shall know that you are not spies but true men. Then I will deliver your brother and you shall trade in the land.' "

Now when they emptied their sacks, behold, every man found his bundle of money in his sack. And when both they and their father saw the bundles of money, they were afraid. Jacob said to them:

"You have taken away my children from me. Joseph is no more, and Simeon is no more, and now you want to take Benjamin away. All these things are against me."

Reuben said to his father:

"You may kill my two sons if I do not bring Benjamin back to you. Put him into my hands, and I will bring him to you again."

But Jacob said: "My son shall not go down with you, for his brother is dead, and he alone is left. If harm should come to him on the journey, you would bring down my gray hairs with sorrow to the grave."

BENJAMIN GOES TO EGYPT

The famine continued in the land. And the time came when Jacob and his sons had eaten up the grain which they had brought from Egypt, and their father said to them:

"Go again, buy us a little food."

But Judah told him:

"If you will send our brother with us, we will go down and buy you food, but if you will not send him, we will not go down, for the man said to us: 'You shall not see my face unless your brother is with you.'"

"Why did you deal so badly with me as to tell the man you had another brother?" asked Jacob.

And they explained:

"The man asked many questions about ourselves and about our family, saying: 'Is your father still alive? Have you another brother?' We answered according to his questions. How could we know that he would say: 'Bring your brother down?'"

Then Judah said to his father Jacob:

"Send the lad with me, and we shall arise and go, so that we may live and not die, we and you and all our little ones.

"I will be responsible for him, and you may demand him of me. If I do not bring him to you and set him before you, then let me bear the blame forever. If we had not lingered so long surely we would already have been back, a second time."

Their father said to them:

"If it must be so now, do this: Take some of the best fruits of the land in your sacks and carry down to the man presents, a little balm, and a little honey, spices and myrrh, nuts and almonds. Take double money in your hands. In this way you will be able to give back the money that

was in the mouths of your sacks. It may be that it was an oversight.

"Take also your brother, and go again to the man. May God Almighty grant you mercy from the man, so that he may send home Benjamin and your other brother Simeon. For if I must grieve for my children, it is bitter grief indeed."

And the men took presents, and they took double money in their hand. They took also Benjamin and started off and went down to Egypt. They came and stood before Joseph.

THE BROTHERS ARE TAKEN TO JOSEPH'S HOUSE

Joseph saw Benjamin with them, and he said to the ruler of his house:

"Take these men home, kill some meat, and make it ready, for these men will dine with me at noon."

The servant did as Joseph told him, and took the brothers to Joseph's house.

The men were afraid when they were brought into Joseph's house, and they said: "It is because of the money that was returned in our sacks the first time that we have been brought here, so that he may find fault with us, and fall upon us, and take us for slaves, and seize our asses."

So they approached the steward of Joseph's house, and they spoke to him in the doorway.

"O Sir," they said, "truly we came down the first time only to buy food, but when we went back and opened our sacks, behold, every man's money was in the mouth of his sack, our money in full amount, so we have brought it back with us.

"We have brought other money down, too, to buy food. We do not know who put the money in our sacks."

"Peace be with you," said the steward. "Fear not. Your God, the God of your father, gave you the treasure in your sacks. I received your money."

Then he brought Simeon out to them.

The man took the brothers into Joseph's house, and he gave them water to wash their feet, and he gave food to their asses. Meanwhile they prepared the presents to give to Joseph when he came in at noon, for they had been told that they were to eat there.

When Joseph came home, they brought him the presents which they had brought into the house, and they bowed themselves down to the earth before him.

He asked them how they were, and said: "Is your father well, the old man of whom you spoke? Is he still alive?"

"Your servant, our father, is in good health," they answered. "He is still alive."

And they bowed down their heads respectfully.

Lifting up his eyes, Joseph saw his brother Benjamin, his own mother's son, and he said:

"Is this the youngest brother of whom you told me?" Then he said: "God be gracious to you, my son."

Then Joseph hurried away, for his heart yearned for his brother, and he sought a place to weep. He went into his room and he wept there. Then he washed his face and calmed himself and went out and said: "Serve the food."

JOSEPH DINES WITH HIS BROTHERS

The servants served him separately and the brothers by themselves, and the Egyptians, who ate also by themselves, because the Egyptians could not eat bread with the Hebrews, for that was against the laws of the Egyptians.

The brothers sat before Joseph in order, from the first-born according to his birthright down to the youngest according to his youth. The men looked at one another in wonderment.

Joseph sent servings to them from his table, and Benjamin's serving was five times as much as any of the others.

They drank and were merry with him.

Then Joseph gave orders to the steward of his house, saying:

"Fill the men's sacks with food as much as they can carry, and put every man's money in his sack's mouth. And put my cup, the silver cup, in the mouth of the sack of the youngest, with his grain money."

The steward did everything Joseph had told him.

As soon as the morning was light, the men were sent away, they and their asses. When they had left the city, but were not yet far off, Joseph said to his steward:

"Up, follow the men! When you have overtaken them, say to them: 'Why have you returned evil for good? Is not this the cup from which my lord drinks, and which he uses in making prophecies? In doing this you have done evil!' "

The steward overtook them, and he spoke to them in the words of Joseph. But they said to him:

"Why does my lord say these things? God forbid that your servant should do anything like this. Behold, the money we found in our sacks' mouths, we brought back to you from the land of Canaan. Why then would we steal silver or gold out of your lord's house?

"Let whoever among us is found to have this object die, and the rest of us will be your lord's slaves."

The steward said:

"Let it be as you say. He who is found to have it shall be my slave, but the rest of you shall be blameless."

Then each man speedily put down his sack on the ground, and each man opened his sack. The steward searched beginning with the eldest and finishing

with the youngest, and the cup was found in Benjamin's sack.

Joseph's brothers tore their clothes in grief; then each man loaded his ass again and they returned to the city.

Judah and his brothers came to Joseph's house and found him there. They fell down before him on the ground. Joseph said to them:

"What is this that you have done? Do you not know that a man like me can see through these things?"

"What shall we say to my lord?" answered Judah. "How shall we speak and how shall we clear ourselves? God has found out the wickedness of your servants. Behold, we shall be my lord's slaves, all of us as well as he in whose sack the cup was found."

"God forbid that I should demand that," Joseph said. "The man in whose hand the cup was found, he shall be my slave. As for the rest of you, go in peace up to your father."

JUDAH PLEADS WITH JOSEPH

Then Judah came closer to him and said: "Oh, my lord, I beg of you, let your servant speak a word in my lord's ear, and do not let your anger burn against your servant, even though you are as powerful as Pharaoh.

"My lord asked his servants: 'Have you a father or a brother?' And we said to my lord: 'We have a father, an old man, and in his old age he had a child, a little boy whose brother is dead, and he alone is left of his mother. His father loves him.'

"Then you said to your servants: 'Bring him down to me, that I may have a look at him.' We said to my lord: 'The lad cannot leave his father, for if he should leave his father, his father would die.' You said to your servants: 'Unless your youngest brother comes down with you, you will not see my face again!'

"So when we came up to your servant, my father, we told him your words. And our father said: 'Go again, and buy us a little food.' We said: 'We cannot go. Only if our youngest brother is with us can we go, for we may not see the man's face if our youngest brother is not with us.'

"And your servant, my father, said to us: 'You know that my wife bore me two sons. One I lost and surely he was torn to pieces. I have not seen him since. If you take this one from me too, and any harm befalls him, you will bring down my gray hairs with sorrow to the grave.'

"Now, therefore, when I come to your servant, my father, and he sees the lad is not with us, his life being bound up with the lad's life, he shall surely die, and your servants will have brought down their father to the grave with sorrow.

"For your servant took upon him responsibility for the lad, saying, 'If I do not bring him back to you, then I shall bear the blame forever.'

"Now therefore, I beg of you, let your servant stay instead of the lad, a slave to my lord. And let the lad go home with his brothers. For how shall I go up to my father if the lad is not with me, and see the grief that would come upon my father?"

JOSEPH REVEALS WHO HE IS

Then Joseph could not restrain himself before all of them that stood around him. He cried:

"Let everyone leave me!" So the Egyptians departed, and Joseph made himself known to his brothers. But he wept aloud, and the Egyptians and Pharaoh's household heard.

Joseph said to his brothers: "I am Joseph. Is my father still alive?"

His brothers could not answer him, for they were all overcome with fear.

Joseph said to his brothers:

"Come close to me, I beg you."

They came near, and he said: "I am Joseph, your brother, whom you sold into Egypt. Now do not grieve nor be angry with yourselves because you sold me here, for God sent me here ahead of you, to save your lives.

"For two years now the famine has been in the land, and there are five more years to come in which there shall be neither tilling nor harvest. God sent me here ahead of you to preserve your families on the earth and to save your lives. Therefore it was not really you that sent me here, but God, and he has made me an adviser to Pharaoh, and lord of his household, and a ruler throughout the land of Egypt.

"Hurry now, and go up to my father, and you will say to him: 'Your son Joseph says: God has made me lord of all Egypt. Come down to me without delay. You shall dwell in the land of Goshen, where you shall be near me, you, your children, and your children's children, your flocks and your herds, and all you own. And I will nourish you here, for there are still five years of famine to come, and you and your household would know poverty otherwise.'

"Now your eyes and the eyes of my brother, Benjamin, can see that it is really I who speak to you. You are to tell my father of all my glory in Egypt, and of all you have seen. Go and hurry, and bring my father down here."

He embraced Benjamin, his brother, and he wept, and Benjamin wept. Then he kissed all his brothers and wept with them, and after that his brothers talked with him.

PHARAOH'S INVITATION

EWS of the event was heard in Pharaoh's house. "Joseph's brothers have come." This pleased Pharaoh well, and his servants were pleased.

Pharaoh said to Joseph:

"Say to your brothers: 'Load your beasts, and go, hurry up to the land of Canaan. Get your father and your households and come to me, and I will give you the best of the land of Egypt, and you shall eat of the fat of the land.' And give these orders: 'Take wagons up from Egypt for your little ones and your wives, and bring your father and come back. Do not bring with you your goods, for the best of all the land of Egypt shall be yours.'"

Therefore Joseph gave his brothers wagons, and gave them provisions for the journey. To each of them he gave changes of clothes, but to Benjamin he gave three hundred pieces of silver and five changes of clothes. To his father he sent these gifts: ten asses loaded with the good things of Egypt, and ten she-asses loaded with corn and bread and meat for his provisions on the journey.

Then he sent his brothers away, and they left. He said to them, "See that you do not have any trouble on the way and do not quarrel."

They went up out of Egypt and

came to the land of Canaan to Jacob their father. They told him all, saying:

"Joseph is still alive! He is the governor over the land of Egypt."

Jacob's heart grew faint, for he could not believe it. But they told him every word Joseph had said to them, and when he saw the wagons which Joseph had sent to carry him, the spirit of Jacob revived. He said:

"It is enough that Joseph my son is still alive. I will go up and see him before I die."

JACOB'S DREAM

JACOB then left for Beer-sheba with everything he owned, and offered sacrifices to the God of his father Isaac.

God spoke to him at night in a dream, saying:

"Jacob, Jacob."

"Here I am," said Jacob.

God said:

"I am the God of your father. Do not fear to go down into Egypt, for I will establish you there as a great nation. I will go down with you into Egypt, and I will surely bring you up again. Joseph shall put his hand upon your eyes."

Jacob departed from Beer-sheba, and his sons carried their father, their little ones and their wives in the wagons which the Pharaoh had sent to carry them. They took their cattle and the goods which they had acquired in the land of Canaan. And so Jacob came into Egypt, and all his kindred with him: his sons and the sons of his sons, his daughters and his sons' daughters. All of them he brought with him into Egypt.

JACOB IN EGYPT

JACOB came into the land of Goshen. And Joseph made ready his chariot and went up to meet his father. He presented himself to him, and he fell on his neck, and he wept on his neck a good while. Jacob said to Joseph:

"Now I may die, since I have seen your face and know you are still alive."

Joseph took five of his brothers and presented them to Pharaoh. And Pharaoh spoke to them saying:

"What is your occupation?" And they answered, "We are shepherds. We pray you, on account of the famine in Canaan, to let us dwell in Goshen." Then Pharaoh turned to Joseph and said: "Your father and your brothers have come to you. The land of Egypt is before you. Have your father and your brothers dwell in the best part of the land of Goshen. If you know any men of great value among them, make them overseers of the cattle that belong to me."

Then Joseph brought in Jacob, his father, and set him before Pharaoh. And Jacob blessed Pharaoh.

115

THE
FAMINE

JOSEPH placed his father and his brothers in the best of the land, in the land of Rameses, as Pharaoh had ordered. Joseph provided his father, his brothers and all his father's household with bread, according to the size of the families.

Now the famine was everywhere very great. Both Egypt and the land of Canaan were exhausted by it. So Joseph gathered from the people all the money that was in the land of Egypt and in the land of Canaan in exchange for the grain that he sold them. Joseph brought the money into Pharaoh's house.

When the money failed in the land of Egypt and in the land of Canaan, all the Egyptians came to Joseph, saying:

"Give us bread! Must we die before your eyes because the money has lost its value?"

Joseph said: "Give your cattle, and I will give you bread for your cattle."

So they brought their cattle and Joseph gave them bread in exchange for horses, flocks and herds, and for asses.

During that year, he fed them with bread in exchange for their cattle. When the year was ended, they came to him the second year, saying to him:

"We will not hide from my lord that, since our money is gone and my lord has our herds of cattle, there is nothing left in the sight of my lord, except our bodies and our land. Why should we die before your eyes, both we and our land?

"Buy us and our land for bread, and we may live and not die and that our land may not be barren."

So Joseph bought all the land of Egypt for Pharaoh. Every Egyptian sold his field, for the famine prevailed over them, and all the land became the

land. When the harvest time comes, you will give the fifth part of the harvest to Pharaoh, and four parts shall be your own for seed for the field and for your food and the food of your little ones."

"You have saved our lives," they said.

"Let us find grace in the sight of my lord, and we will be the servants of Pharaoh."

Joseph made it a law over the land of Egypt that Pharaoh should have the fifth part from the harvest of the land, except from the land of the priests.

property of Pharaoh. The people he removed to cities from one end of the border of Egypt to the other.

Only the priests kept their lands, for Pharaoh had assigned them a portion of food, and they lived on the portion Pharaoh had given them.

The priests therefore did not sell their lands.

And Joseph said to the people:

"Now, I have bought you and your land for Pharaoh. So, here is seed for you, and you shall sow the

Jacob lived in the land of Egypt for seventeen years, until he became a very old man. And when he was about to die, he called his son Joseph and said:

"If I have found grace in your sight, deal kindly and truly with me. Do not bury me in Egypt, I pray you. Let me lie with my fathers. Carry me out of Egypt and bury me in their burying place.

"Bury me where they buried Abraham and Sarah his wife, where they buried Isaac and Rebekah his wife, and where I buried Leah."

Joseph said:

"I will do as you have said."

"Swear to do as I wish," said Jacob.

Joseph swore to him, and Jacob bowed himself upon the bed's head. Then he said to Joseph:

"Behold, I will die soon! But God shall be with you and will bring you again to the land of your fathers."

Then Jacob called his twelve sons and said:

"Gather yourselves together, that I may tell you what will happen to you in the days to come. Gather, and hear me, sons of Jacob, and hear Israel your father."

Jacob, who was called Israel, told how the twelve tribes of Israel would descend from his twelve sons. And he spoke to each of the sons in turn: Reuben, Simeon, Levi, Judah, Issachar, Zebulun, Benjamin, Dan, Naphthali, Gad, Joseph and Asher. He foretold that Judah's tribe would be the one which all the others would praise, bowing down before it. And he blessed every son with a blessing.

Then Jacob gathered up his feet into the bed and yielded up the ghost and was united with his people.

Joseph fell upon his father's face, and wept upon him, and kissed him. Then he commanded his servants, the physicians, to embalm his father.

The physicians embalmed Israel and then the Egyptians mourned for him threescore and ten days.

When the days of mourning were past, Joseph spoke to the house of Pharaoh, saying:

"If I have found grace in your

eyes, speak, I pray you, in the ears of Pharaoh and say that my father made me swear to bury him in the grave he dug for himself in the land of Canaan. Therefore, may Pharaoh let me go up, I pray, and bury my father and then I will come again."

Pharaoh said:

"Go up and bury your father, according to his wishes."

JOSEPH BURIES HIS FATHER

So Joseph went up to bury his father, and with him went all the servants of Pharaoh, the elders of his house, and all the elders of the land of Egypt, all the household. Only the little ones, their flocks and their herds did they leave in the land of Goshen. Also chariots and horsemen went up with him. It was a very great caravan.

They came to the threshing-floor of Atad, which is beyond Jordan. There they mourned with great and sorrowing cries. For seven days Joseph mourned for his father.

Then Jacob's sons carried their father into the land of Canaan, as he had commanded. They buried him in the cave of the field of Machpelah.

After his father was buried, Joseph returned to Egypt, he and his brothers and all that went up with him to bury his father.

Now that their father was dead, Joseph's brothers said:

"If Joseph should ever hate us, he would surely make return for all the evil we did to him."

So they sent a messenger to Joseph, saying:

"Before his death, your father spoke to us, saying: 'You shall say to Joseph: Forgive the trespass of your brothers and the sin which they committed when they did evil to you.'"

Joseph wept when they spoke to

him. And his brothers went to him and fell down before his face, and said:

"Behold, we are your servants!"

"Fear not," said Joseph. "Am I here in the place of God? You meant evil against me, but God meant to turn it to good and to bring to pass what is today: to keep many people alive.

"Therefore have no fear. I will nourish you, you and your little ones."

Then he comforted them and spoke kindly to them.

JOSEPH DIES

Thereafter, Joseph dwelt in Egypt, he and his father's house.

He lived to see Ephraim's and Manasseh's children and grandchildren. And when he was one hundred and ten years old, Joseph said to his brothers:

"God will surely visit you after my death, and bring you out of this land, into the land which he promised to Abraham, to Isaac, and to Jacob."

And Joseph exacted a promise from the children of Israel, saying: "God will surely visit you, and you shall carry my bones from here."

Joseph was an old man when he died, but less old than his father had been. He was embalmed and put in a coffin in Egypt.

ILLUSTRATED
GLOSSARY

Balm (p. 92)

Balm is used to soothe and heal wounds. It is made from the "balm of Gilead," a tree which grows in the hills of Gilead, east of the Jordan River.

Beersheba (p. 80)

Beersheba was a town at the southernmost point of Canaan. When Abraham first stopped there, it was a small oasis. He dug a well under its palm trees to obtain water for his family and animals. Later, his son Isaac dug wells there too.

The ancient Hebrews said their country stretched from Dan to Beersheba, a distance of about 150 miles from north to south.

Birthright (p. 74)

During biblical times, after a man died all his possessions were divided among his sons; daughters had no rights if there were boys in the family. However, the oldest son received twice as much as any of his brothers. A son's right to inheritance was called his birthright. As the older son, Esau had the right to inherit twice as much of Isaac's wealth as his brother Jacob.

Cave of Machpelah (p. 119)

Located near Hebron, a city west of the Dead (Salt) Sea, the cave of Machpelah was used as a burial place for many of the patriarchs. Abraham bought the field of Machpelah and its cave from Ephron, a Hittite. He buried his wife Sarah there. Later he was buried beside her, and his son Isaac shepherded his flocks in the pastures nearby. Jacob wished to be buried there beside his grandparents, so

Joseph carried his body there and mourned him.

Chariot (p. 99)

The Israelites, Egyptians, and other peoples of biblical lands went to battle in light, two-wheeled, open carts called chariots. Fast horses were used to pull the chariots.

A chariot often carried three people to battle: the driver, the archer or bowman, and the shield-bearer. It was the shield-bearer's duty to hold a large shield before the other two to protect them from enemy arrows. This left the archer free to use both hands for his bow and arrow.

Embalm (p. 118)

In Egypt, where people believed in an afterlife that would be exactly like this life, dead bodies were preserved by a process called embalming. The body was treated with certain substances that would preserve it and prepare it for the afterlife.

The Hebrews did not usually practice embalming. Yet we read that Joseph had his father embalmed, and that later his own body was treated in the same way. Probably Joseph and his family had lived so long among the Egyptians that he had adopted some of their customs. Then, too, the Egyptians may have insisted that the bodies be embalmed.

Famine (p. 98)

A famine occurs when food is scarce for many years and people are near starvation. The very dry weather of a long rainless period is usually the cause of a famine, because crops cannot grow and cattle die of thirst and starvation.

Although rain almost never falls directly in Egypt, the food supply is usually good because the Nile River carries water from less arid regions.

Although the Canaan region is also a hot dry land, rain falls there in spring and autumn. The Hebrews dug many wells, but the well water sometimes failed during very dry periods. Then famine would strike. It was during such a famine that Jacob went down into Egypt with his sons.

Goshen (p. 111)

The land of Goshen was an area in the northern part of Egypt. It stretched from east of the Nile Delta to what is now the Suez Canal. Crops flourished in the delta, and it was the Egyptians' prime farmland. The land east of the delta was poor for farming, but was perfect pasture land. The Hebrews were given this good land as a grazing place for their cattle.

Lentils (p. 74)

Lentils are flat round seeds of a vegetable belonging to the same family as peas and beans. The Hebrew people grew lentils and this high-protein food was especially popular among the poor. Lentils were used as a vegetable, for making soup, and were even ground up to make flour for bread.

Some scholars think lentils were the first vegetable that people grew. Archaeologists found lentils in big stone jars when they excavated at Jericho. The seeds had been stored there five thousand years before, and were still in good condition.

Myrrh (p. 92)

Myrrh is made from gum taken from the bark of a spiny shrub called rock rose. It has a pleasant fragrance and is used for perfumes and incense.

Padan-Aram (p. 78)

Padan-Aram was a flat area in the northern part of Mesopotamia. Its name means "the plain of Aram." Aram was a son of Shem, and a grandson of Noah. The city of Haran, Abraham's home, was located close to the center of Padan-Aram.

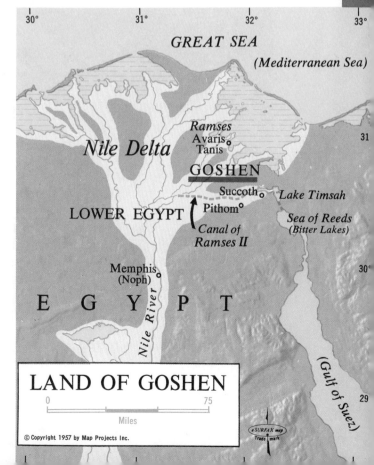

GREAT SEA
(Mediterranean Sea)

Nile Delta
Ramses
Avaris
Tanis
GOSHEN
Succoth
Lake Timsah
LOWER EGYPT
Pithom
Sea of Reeds
(Bitter Lakes)
Canal of
Ramses II
Memphis
(Noph)
E G Y P T
Nile River
(Gulf of Suez)

LAND OF GOSHEN

0   75
Miles

© Copyright 1957 by Map Projects Inc.

The Hebrew shepherds stopped at oasises like this to get drinking water for themselves and for their flocks.

Pharaoh (p. 94)

The pharaoh was a king or ruler of Egypt. It is likely that the pharaoh during Joseph's first years in Egypt was descended from a partly Semitic people who had invaded Egypt.

Quiver (p. 75)

Arrows are carried in a quiver, a container that looks like a small golf bag. In biblical times a quiver was usually hung on a long cord worn over one shoulder. The cord crossed the body so that the quiver was held near the waist, where the arrows were easily reached.

When a bowman hunted with a bow and arrow, or when he went to war, he carried a quiver. If he rode to battle in a chariot, the quiver was carried over the chariot's side.

Sackcloth (p. 92)

The dark coarse cloth made from the hair of goats and camels was called sackcloth because it was meant to be sewn into bags or sacks. It was used as a garment by those mourning the death of a loved one. Mourners also sprinkled ashes on their heads.

Steward (p. 106)

A person who was placed in charge of a household or a piece of property was called a steward. The steward of Joseph's house was a head servant who, most likely, was in charge of the other servants, of all the food and supplies that went into the house, and of keeping the house clean and in good repair.

Threshing-floor (p. 119)

Threshing is the first step in getting grain ready to be made into flour. The grains of wheat are removed from their stalks on a large, round floor called a threshing-floor.

In biblical times a threshing-floor was either paved with stone or made of hard-packed earth. It was owned by everyone in the village who raised wheat or barley.

After the stalks had been cut they were carried to the floor in bundles, either on the backs of animals or in carts. A large, heavy slab of wood that had rows of sharp stones or pieces of metal on its underside was used to crush the stalks.

An ox or an ass was hitched to this threshing board and either a grown person or a child sat upon it and drove the work animal. Round and round the floor the board would go. As it moved over the wheat, the sharp teeth on the underside loosened the grains and cut the stalks into short pieces.

"Water to wash their feet" (p. 106)

It was a custom among the Hebrews and other Eastern peoples to offer guests water to wash their feet. As soon as a guest arrived, after a tiring journey on foot along dusty, unpaved roads, his host would bring a bowl of water and a towel to him. With these the guest's feet were washed. Then the host rubbed perfumed oil on his guest's forehead or hair. To omit such gestures was considered rude.